PRAYER

WHEN

ALL SEEMS

LOST

By Tella Olayeri

08023583168

Email; tellaolayeri@gmail.com

Website www.tellaolayeri.com

US Contact

Ruth Jack

14 Milewood Road

Verbank

N.Y.12585

U.S.A. +19176428989

DEDICATION

This book is dedicated to **HOLY GHOST** for inspiring me to write this eye opener book.

APPRECIATION

My appreciation goes to my dedicated wife, **MRS NGOZI OLAYERI,** who typed the manuscript of this book and designed the cover page.

My appreciation also goes to my lovely children, **MISS IBUKUN, DAVID, MICHAEL, COMFORT and MERCY.** They encouraged me day and night as I write this book.

Respect and honour should be given to who is due. Favour comes from God and men as well. My calling (writing evangelism) met timely support of a man of God, preacher, teacher, prophet and General Overseer. He awakes my inner man and gave me sound spiritual support. Without his earlier support for my first book, *Fire for Fire Prayer Book* and subsequent ones, I may not be where I am today in Christian literature writing. He gallantly stood by me in fulfillment of my calling.

This book you are holding is a testimony of my claim. This book wouldn't have seen the light of the day, if not for the spiritual encouragement I gathered from my father in the Lord who served as spiritual mirror that brightens my hope to explore my calling.

I am talking of no any other person than the **General Overseer of *MOUNTAIN OF FIRE AND MIRACLES MINISTRIES WORLD WIDE*, DR. D. K. OLUKOYA.**

Once again, I say thank you sir. Your support has yielded yet another earth shaking book.
THANKS
Evangelist Tella Olayeri.

PREFACE

Emergency phone call is crucial in our daily endeavour. Every link with God, open doors of easy communication and direction. It makes life easy as you take right step in the right direction. Failure seems far, fear is defeated while arrogance of the enemy is checkmated. If you call and God hears, you are close to success.

All these, emergency phone numbers, can be found in heavenly directory; the Holy Bible; and its Author may be dialed direct. There is no gain saying, you do it with ease. No operator assistance is needed or necessary. All lines to heaven are open 24 hours a day! This is the reason, emergency numbers are available.

It is time you test your faith. God is willing to hear from you, willing to answer you. He is ready to fulfill his promise with us as stated in Isaiah 1:18. **"Come now, let us reason together" says the LORD. "Though your sins are like scarlet, they shall be as white as snow; though they are red as crimson, they shall be like wool."** God cannot weigh or look at your sin as too much or many. He is willing to discard them all, if only you look unto him for forgiveness and do away with sins. At such spot, if you call him, he will hear and answer. Therefore, build faith like mustard seed, and come to God. Feed your faith, and doubt will starve to death!

The fact is, you are qualified to use emergency phone call of God without favour. It has been tested by many with results to show for it. You mustn't allow Satan to rob you your right. Cast doubt aside, your sins are forgiven if you reason with God. Your chains are broken, enjoy freedom from fetters of darkness God breaks, it shall not rear its ugly head second time.

Is your faith going down? Is your prayer becoming narrow and narrow? Are you dejected? Do you harbour sorrow in the heart? Are you depressed? Do you experience holes in the pocket? Do you lose confidence people on friends and family alike? Do people seem unkind to you? Does your work place hunts you? This and many issues are discussed in depth here to save you from situations you find yourself.

God bless you as you read on.

GOOD NEWS!!!

My audiobook is now available. To get one go to acx.com and search **Tella Olayeri**.

Thanks.

PREVIOUS PUBLICATIONS OF THE AUTHOR

1. *Fire for Fire Prayer Book Part 1*
2. *Fire for Fire Prayer Book Part 2*
3. *My Marriage Shall Not Break*
4. *Prayer for Pregnant Women*
5. *Prayer for the Fruit of the Womb*
6. *Children Deliverance*
7. *Prayer for Youths and Teenagers*
8. *Prayer for Singles*
9. *Victory over Satanic House Part 1*
10. *Victory over Satanic House Part 2*
11. *I Shall Excel*
12. *Atomic Prayers that Destroy Witchcraft Powers and Silence Enemies*
13. *Goliath at the Gate of Marriage*
14. *Deliverance from Spirit of Dogs*
15. *Naked Warriors*
16. *Prayer Against Sex in the Dream*
17. *Strange Women! Leave My Husband Alone*
18. *Dangerous Prayer against Strange Women*
19. *630 Acidic Prayer Points*
20. *Power to Retain Job and Excel in Office*
21. *Warfare in the Office*
22. *Command the Year*
23. *Deliverance Prayer for First Born*
24. *800 Deliverance Prayer for First Born Part Two*
25. *Prayer for Good Health and Divine Healing*
26. *Prayer against Untimely Death.*
27. *Dictionary of Dreams*

Table of Contents

CHAPTER ONE

WHEN YOU THINK OF INVESTMENTS AND RETURNS…CALL MARK 10

There is time for investments and time for returns. An investor expects returns from investment no matter how little. Investors raise eye brow when they invest and couldn't get returns from what they invested. It goes thus; when you pray and fast (Spiritual investment) you expect answer (physical manifestation). When you sow, you expect to reap. The truth of the matter is, before you sow, phone God. It is also wise to call the emergency phone number of God, when you sow or invest but couldn't get returns at due time. If this is so, call Mark 10. This is the emergency phone number of God in such a situation.

Strive hard to keep your marriage intact; it is a source of strength that enlarges marital coast. Children are product of marriage that brings joy to mind. Your wealth should take you to heaven not hell. You that invest in the Lord shall not reap failure. No one trades with God and regret doing it.

When you invest in marriage, you expect marital bliss; fruitful marriage with blessed children, peaceful home that abhor divorce. Blissful marriage entails fruitful career as well. We should surrender our marriage, calling and career to the Lord Almighty for blessing and fruitfulness. When God is in charge, whatever we lay hands upon is blessed. Our spirit glues to God for eternity, the ultimate race on earth. Our moral standard is sharpening along with commandment of God, making us love our neighbour as our self. When you invest goodness on your neighbour, you get heavenly returns. No matter what, don't allow treasure on earth blindfold you against heavenly rest.

We should take notice of one thing. It is not all emergency calls God listens to; even if you do his work whole heart. No matter the fasting and prayer you go through, God may say, "No, it is not time, meanwhile to you, time is ripe. Really, the time may not be right now, until confirmed by God. If you ignore God's confirmation and invest, you may reap failure; even in the works of God.

The book of Act 16:6 gives clear account of time investment **"They were forbidden of the Holy Ghost to preach the Word in Asia"** It wasn't ripe then to preach in Asia. If they haven't yield to the Holy Spirit's prohibition, they may reap failure. The work is to be done by Paul in years to come not now. There, Paul would do some of the greatest work of his life, but just now the door was closed against him by the Holy Spirit. The kingdom of Satan in this region shall be dealt with in years to come. Meanwhile, Apollos must come there for pioneer work. Paul and Barnabass are needed yet more urgently elsewhere, and must receive further training before undertaking this responsible task.

If you invest wisely, beggarly spirit shall depart your life, giving room for heavenly visions. The veil that held you captive shall disappear. The Bible said of Jesus when he heard the cry of blind Bartimeaus, he stood still. **"And Jesus stood still, and commanded him to be called..."** Mark 10:49. The cry of blind Bartimaeus arrested Jesus. He was like one glued to a spot for action. Heaven got attention of the cry of Bartimaeus his cry (investment), got instant answer (returns). Hence, I pray, in every emergency situation you find yourself, the Lord Almighty shall hear your cry and answer you.

The way you treat and accept situation matters a lot. There are times God is with us, but for fear and doubts we lose out; what we invest fail woefully.

When God opens your eyes you see how he helps. In the face of physical defeat God is there taking you to glorious end. Only pray for open eyes to see what awaits you at the other end. In the midst of victory, the servant of Elisha prayed, and said, **"Lord, I pray thee; open his eyes, that he may see"** 2 Kings 6:17.

This is the prayer to pray and for others. "Lord, open our eyes that we may see". The world around us is full of God's horses and chariots waiting to carry us to places of glorious victory. And when our eyes are thus open, we see events of life; investments so far invested, and returns gathered so far, whether great or small, whether joyful or sad, a "Chariot" for our souls.

Our journey in life lies with each of us to choose which they shall be. It all depends, not upon what these events are, but upon how we take them. If we lie down under them, and let them roll over us and crush us, they become killer cars, but if we climb up into them, as into a car of victory, and make them carry us triumphantly onward and upward, they become the chariots of God.

Prayer alone is not enough to address emergency situation; try and hear from God. When you hear from author of life, you hardly miss it. Holy Spirit whispers to our ears, only we most often ignore him, using carnal wisdom instead. There is joy in obeying Holy Spirit. He guides as perfect master.

It is said, obedience is better than sacrifice. Obedience of Peter to Jesus instruction catapulted him to greater height. Jesus said; cast your net into the water for a catch, even though you caught nothing for so long. Peter obeyed, and caught net breaking harvest.

Peter was at a critical point of loss. It was as if the days have defeated him. No catch of fish all the night long. Jesus met Peter at day time when fishes have withdrawn far into the sea. In fact, they are about to wash the net and call it a day, when Jesus appeared. The appearance of Jesus in this scene changed Peter's destiny. I pray, at the point you lost hope, thinking all is gone, Jesus shall appear in your life. At every eleventh hour, your saviour shall appear, in the name of Jesus.

When God appears in your life, protocol is broken. Climate change in your favour, capital liquidity threat bows, and debtor's inability to pay ends, while creditors scramble to help you; all because the Master is around. In time of emergency the Master shall provide adequate facility to address your situations. When God's hand is on your business or career, fruitfulness follows.

I pray that power of fruitfulness shall not depart in your life. Amen.

PRAYER POINTS

1. O Lord, appear in my situation and let protocol be broken to favour me in the name of Jesus.

2. When climate is against me, it shall favour me, in the name of Jesus.

3. My bank account improve and favour me for expansion in the name of Jesus.

4. O Lord, touch the heart of debtors to pay me without question or quarrel in the name of Jesus.

5. My helpers arise, locate me and help me in the name of Jesus.

6. My father and my God, breathe breath of life into my career, in the name of Jesus.

7. At every critical point where hope is lost my God shall arise and see me through in the name of Jesus.

8. Everyday shall favour me, no day shall defeat me in the name of Jesus.

9. O Lord, anoint the works of my hands, where I toiled and fail, convert it to success.

10. O Lord, use supernatural magnet to magnetise my virtues in the hands of the enemy to me, in the name of Jesus.

11. I will not call it a day, when my success is about to manifest in the name of Jesus.

12. Lord Jesus, appear at critical point, in my life, when my hope is almost lost.

13. My destiny, attract Jesus and be blessed in the name of Jesus.

14. O Lord, open my inner ear to carry out your instruction in the name of Jesus.

15. Holy Spirit divine, lay hands upon me for new anointing, in the name of Jesus.

16. Spirit of obedience dwell in me in the name of Jesus.

17. Holy Spirit, Perfect Master, make my ways perfect in the name of Jesus.

18. Lord Jesus, appear in my life, open my eyes to see what surrounds me.

19. Horses and chariots of God carry me to glorious position in the name of Jesus.

20. I shall not cry when I should laugh in the name of Jesus.

21. Beggar spirit in my life, come out and die in the name of Jesus.

22. Satanic veil in my face, clear away and be removed in the name of Jesus.

23. O Lord, give me power to sow and reap in the name of Jesus.

24. I cry you O Lord, answer me without delay in the order of blind Bartimaeus.

25. My investment, receive heavenly fertilizer in the name of Jesus.

26. My investment shall not be a failure in the name of Jesus.

27. My eyes shall see the defeat of my enemies in the name of Jesus.

28. O Lord, crown me with crown of glory in the name of Jesus.

29. O Lord, restore my lost hope in the name of Jesus.

30. Lord Jesus, I surrender my home to you, bless us by your power.

31. My career, be blessed in the name of Jesus.

32. O Lord, enlarge my coast, make me smile and laugh at last, in the name of Jesus.

CHAPTER TWO

WHEN YOUR FAITH NEEDS STIRRING…CALL HEBREWS 11

There is no shortcut to life of faith, which is the all-vital condition of a holy and victorious life. You never learn faith in comfortable surroundings. Faith is not bread and butter approach to life, you must build it. Faith is built in us, by us to stand firm before the Lord.

How does faith works? God give us the promises in a quiet hour, God seals our covenants with great and gracious words, and then lets the tempter come, and the test seems to contradict all that he has spoken. It is then that faith wins its crown.

When faith claims promises of God it becomes prophecy and we go forth feeling that it is something that must be done because God cannot lie. Faith turns the promise into prophecy. When you build on the promises of God, your faith becomes higher. Faith is seeing as an actual fact that God has said that this thing shall come to pass, and that it is true, and then rejoicing to know that it is true, and just resting because God has said it.

Faith requires sacrifice. We must burn out before we can give out. We cease to bless when we cease to bleed. That bleed is sacrifice that yields. Poverty, hardship and misfortune have pressed many a life to moral heroism and spiritual greatness. Difficulty challenges energy and perseverance. It calls into activity the strongest qualities of the soul. All these come about as a result of faith.

Many characters in the Bible were bruised, threshed and ground into bread for the hungry. Abraham acquire the degree of being called "the father of the faithful" that was because he gallantly stood at the head of his class in affliction and obedience. The likes of Abraham are many. Jacob suffered threshing and grindings. He became father of twelve tribes of Israel. Joseph was bruised and beaten and had to go through Potiphar's kitchen and Egypt's prison to get to his throne. David hunted like a partridge on the mountain bruised and weary. He became ideal King of Israel. Paul never could have been bread for Caesar's household if he had not endured the bruising, whippings and stoning. He was ground into fine flour for the royal family. It is said, a soul sorely bruised is a soul elect.

Faith is chain events. In our training in the faith – life there must be room for the trial of faith, and often many stages are passed before we really realize what is the end of faith, namely, the victory of faith.

When you have made your request of God, but the answer does not come, what are you to do? The answer is, keep on believing God's word; never be moved away from it by what you see or feel, and thus as you stand steady, enlarged power and experience is being developed. Being unmoved from your position of faith makes you stronger on every other line. In the lives of all the great Bible characters, Abraham, Moses and Elijah were not great in the beginning, but were made great through the discipline of their faith. At last, they were fitted to the positions to which God had called them.

The book of Hebrews 11:1 gives clue as to what is faith. **"Now faith is being sure of what we hope for and certain of what we do not see"**. This is faith for you. But then, we hear men praying everywhere for more faith, but when we listen to them carefully, and get at the real heart of their prayer, very often it is not more faith they are wanting, but a change from faith to sight.

To understand well, we shall ask, what do we mean by faith? Faith is the telegraphic wire which links earth to heaven, on which God's messages of love fly so fast that before we call, he answers and while we are yet speaking he hears us. Faith is powerful. Take faith away, in vain we call to God. There is no other road between us and heaven. It is faith that links us to divinity, because with faith we pray and call upon God.

What is faith? It is what makes us march triumphant over the necks of enemies. With faith we defy the enemy and stand like gallant soldier. By this, we can't be beaten by the enemy.

What is faith? It is what clothes us with the power of Jehovah. Faith empowers us to move forward in life with no fear of attack. It is as if dressed in military outfit that cause fear in the minds of enemies.

What is faith? Faith grows little by little. Abraham went step by step, not by great leaps. The finest jewels are most carefully cut and polished; the hottest fires try the most precious metal.

What is faith? Faith insures every attribute of God in our defense. Faith honours God, God honours faith. With faith, his Omniscience is felt in our undertakings. We felt his presence wherever we go, meaning he is Omnipresent. He is immortal and so we call on him as a living God.

What is faith? Faith is a supernatural faulty which when exercised, brings the unseen into plain view. Faith deals with supernatural. It is by which the impossible things are made possible. Faith grows amid storms caused by confides of the elements. It is when there is disturbance in the spiritual atmosphere, storm arises. In the face of storms faith grows. In such atmosphere faith finds its most productive soil. In the face of conflicts of elements, faith comes more quickly to fruition.

Faith doesn't grow without storm. Every storm tests faith. The question is, do you have faith like mustard seed? Do you have faith like father Abraham? But then, how can we define Abraham's faith? Abraham believed God, and said to sight, "Stand back!" and to the laws of nature, "Hold your peace!" and to a misgiving heart, "Silence, thou lying tempter!" He believed God and walk with God. This is faith.

Therefore, brethren, in the midst of storm don't lose hope, rather build faith. Don't take it as a point of withdrawal or emergency that swallows destiny. The staunchest tree is not found in the shelter of the forest, but one in the open where the winds from every quarter beat upon it, and bend and twist it until it becomes a giant in stature. Imagine, this is the tree which the machine wants his tools made of, and the wagon maker seeks! Storm strengthens the tree, faith makes it grow.

PRAYER POINTS

1. O Lord, give me faith that moves mountain, in the name of Jesus.

2. Faith in me swallow tests of Satan, in the name of Jesus.

3. Troubles that shakes one to deny God, in my life, die in the name of Jesus.

4. Every hole in my pocket assign to kill my faith, expire in the name of Jesus.

5. Arrow of darkness that test faith backfire in the name of Jesus.

6. Every test ahead of me, I overcome you in the name of Jesus.

7. Evil plantation in my life, wither and die in the name of Jesus.

8. Rivers of darkness assign to drown my faith, dry up, in the name of Jesus.

9. At every quiet time my faith shall grow in the name of Jesus.

10. No matter what, my faith shall not die in the name of Jesus.

11. Faith of David, that made him kill Goliath locate me in the name of Jesus.

12. Faith that strengthen Joseph against immorality, fall upon me in the name of Jesus.

13. Faith that makes father Abraham be father of nation fall upon me in the name of Jesus.

14. Every Red Sea on my way to kill my faith, dry up in the name of Jesus.

15. Spirit of impossibility boasting I will fall by wayside, you are a liar, die in the name of Jesus.

16. Every storm in my life, scatter in the name of Jesus.

17. I shall not take reverse steps, where I will make progress in the name of Jesus.

18. Destiny killers assign against me die in the name of Jesus.

19. No matter the bends and twists, my faith is unshakeable in the name of Jesus.

20. Powers against my faith stand back, hold your peace and be silenced in the name of Jesus.

21. Hidden vision in my life come alive in the name of Jesus.

22. No matter the storm, my faith grows amidst storm in the name of Jesus.

23. Supernatural of faith, insure my faith against failure in the name of Jesus.

24. My faith shall not diminish from faith to sight, in the name of Jesus.

25. Faith shall make me march triumphant over the necks of enemies in the name of Jesus.

26. My faith shall pass trials and fires of life in the name of Jesus.

27. As Abraham trust in the Lord, even into the unknown, empower me to trust in you O Lord, in the name of Jesus.

28. Arrows of spiritual impotence, backfire in the name of Jesus.

29. Anti-revival spirit that kills faith, holding me captive, die in the name of Jesus.

30. O Lord, visit me, build my leaking faith in the name of Jesus.

31. My picture in the altar of darkness, I withdraw you in the name of Jesus.

32. O Lord, arise, defend your interest in my life in the name of Jesus.

33. Fire of God, refine, build and energize my faith in the name of Jesus.

CHAPTER THREE

WHEN YOUR PRAYER GROW NARROW...CALL PSALM 67

It is said, prayer answereth all things while prayerlessness brings nothing. When we know this, why is it prayer grows narrow in our lives? It mostly occurs when answer tarries, or when we pray with unbeliever, or indulge in sin pretending as saint.

It is no doubt; prayer grows narrow when the mind is loaded with doubt, fear, failure, temptation, sin, weakness or when under attack. Attack may be spiritual or physical. Daniel found himself in emergency situation and prayed to God. Despite his aggressiveness in prayer the angel was barred from bringing answer. There was a special attack of Satan. The prince of Persia was at work.

Mind you, Daniel fasted and prayed for twenty-one days, and had a very hard time to receive answer. If you read the narrative, Daniel 10:12-13, it wasn't that, Daniel wasn't a good man, nor that his prayer wasn't right, but because of special attack of Satan. Daniel received answer the moment he began to pray, but an evil angel met with good angel and wrestled. There was conflict in the heavens, and Daniel seems to go through an agony on earth waiting for answer. It was a serious emergency time.

No matter what it takes, when a matter requires definite prayer, pray till you receive answer. Don't grow weary, apply instrument of prayer to bring situation under control. Avoid doubt as you pray. Rather than doubt, tell God you are waiting and that you still believe him. Praise him for the answer yet to come. Never center your thought on doubt, believe in God's promise for you. Doing this, you shall pray yourself into faith. Let anxiety and doubt dwell not in you. The beginning of anxiety is the end of faith and the beginning of true faith is the end of anxiety.

Are you tired and overwhelmed with difficulties, trials and emergency. They are all divinely provided vessels for the Holy Spirit to fill, and if you but rightly understand their meanings, they become opportunities for receiving new blessing and deliverance which you can get in no other way. The very trials that threatened to overcome you with discouragement and disaster will become God's opportunity for the revelation of his grace and glory in your life.

Emergency doesn't mean defeat. You may be discouraged but don't give up. Many a Christians' prayer is hindered by Satan, but you shouldn't fear when prayer and faith pile up. After a while they will be like flood, and will not only sweep the answer through but will also bring some new accompanying blessing. What more? The rarest souls have been tested with high pressures and temperatures, but heaven will not desert them.

The man who forms the habit of beginning without finishing has simply formed the habit of failure. The man who begins to pray about a thing and doesn't pray it through to a successful issue of answer has formed the same habit in prayer.

One may then ask, how long shall we pray? Do we not come to a place where we may cease from our petitions and rest the matter in God's hands? There is but one answer. Pray until the thing you pray for has actually been granted, or until you have the assurance in your heart that it will be. Prayer is not only a calling upon God, but also a conflict with Satan. And in as much as God is using our intercession as a mighty factor of victory in that conflict, he alone, and not we, must decide when we dare cease from our petitioning. So we dare not stay our prayer until the answer itself has come, or until we receive the assurance that it will come.

We faint and cease altogether from prayer concerning it when we begin to pray for a certain thing a day, a week, a month, with no definite answer. Our prayer becomes narrow. It is always the snare of many beginnings with no completions. It is ruinous with multiple disadvantage to life.

There are promises that kindle fire in a life. You mustn't surrender to circumstances and allow your prayer grow narrow. The more you pray, better it is.

With promises in the Bible your answer transcend from asking to fulfillment. The following passages in the Bible shall build your faith and enlarge your expectation to fulfillment. Let's look at them one at a time.

Isaiah 65:24. **"Before they call I will answer; while they are still speaking I will hear".**

Jeremiah 33:3. **"Call unto me, and I will answer thee and show thee great and mighty things".**

John 15:7 **"Ask what ye will, and it shall be done unto you".**

Psalm 81:10b. **"Open thy mouth wide, and I will fill it".**

Psalm 34:17. **"The righteous cry (pray), and the Lord heareth, and delivereth them out of all their troubles".**

Psalm 91:15. **"He shall call upon me, and I will answer him".**

Proverb 3:6. **"In all thy ways acknowledge him, and he shall direct thy paths".**

Psalm 50:15 **"Call upon me in the day of trouble: I will deliver thee and thou shalt glorify me"**.

James 5:13. **"Is any among you afflicted? Let him pray"**.

1 Thessalonians 5:17. **"Pray without ceasing"**.

Prayer is not imagination. If a man dreams that he can become mighty in prayer just as he pleases, he labours under a great mistake. It is good to have constant communion with God. Let us never imagine that Abraham could have interceded so successfully for Sodom if he had not been all his lifetime in the practice of communion with God. Therefore, we must pray to pray, and continue in prayer that our prayers may continue.

Hence, let's go into the act of prayer.

PRAYER POINTS

1. Power to pray fall upon me in the name of Jesus.

2. My prayers ascend to heaven and bring results in the name of Jesus.

3. Powers that discourage one to pray quit my life in the name of Jesus.

4. O Lord, turn me to prayer machine in the name of Jesus.

5. Spirit of prayer warrior and warlord possess me by fire in the name of Jesus.

6. Doubts that kill prayer, my heart is not for you, come out and die in the name of Jesus.

7. Arrow of fear fired against me backfire in the name of Jesus.

8. Every arrow of failure fired into my life, backfire in the name of Jesus.

9. Every temptation assign to draw me from prayer, die in the name of Jesus.

10. O Lord, forgive me of sins that keep me down, rather than pray, in the name of Jesus.

11. Fire of baptism prayer possess me in the name of Jesus.

12. Powers that debar my angel from bringing me answer die in the name of Jesus.

13. Prince of Persia attacking my heavenly answer die in the name of Jesus.

14. I possess instruments of prayer to bring fruitfulness in prayer, in the name of Jesus.

15. Power to praise God and receive answer fall upon me in the name of Jesus.

16. Promise of God shall be fulfilled in my life in the name of Jesus.

17. Spirit of anxiety quit my life, prayer shall not elude me in the name of Jesus.

18. Every difficulty assign to bring me down, receive heavenly solution in the name of Jesus.

19. Let every emergency situation receive right answer in the name of Jesus.

20. Prayers that bring blessings and deliverances possess me in the name of Jesus.

21. O Lord, convert my trial to trump in the name of Jesus.

22. Every disaster on my way to success, scatter in the name of Jesus.

23. O Lord, baptise and crown my destiny with grace and favour.

24. Fear of untimely death that hinders prayer expire in the name of Jesus.

25. My pile up prayer and faith, manifest to multiple answer and blessings in the name of Jesus.

26. High pressures and temperatures enemy use to test me become nothing now, for my prayer to receive answer.

27. What I begin, I shall finish well in the name of Jesus.

28. Before I call, O Lord, answer me in the name of Jesus.

29. When I speak, O Lord, hear me and do your will for me in the name of Jesus.

30. O Lord, I open my mouth wide, fill it with answer in the name of Jesus.

31. O Lord, deliver me out of all troubles, in the name of Jesus.

32. I kick out and pray against afflictions in the name of Jesus.

33. O Lord, make me a prayer warlord, to pray and to pray until I get answer. Amen.

CHAPTER FOUR

WHEN THE WORLD SEEMS BIGGER THAN GOD...CALL PSALM 90

When hope is lost and it seems all doors seems close against you, it is like the world bigger than God. You said much prayer, yet it seems answer is not forth coming. You fasted, but seems problem is becoming harder and harder. Everyone you run to for help never welcome you or your idea. They frown at whatever you table before them. At times, their words chase you far more because what they 'vomit' from the mouth is disgusting.

There is hopelessness from every direction. Hopes are as far as sky above. Hope is lost, before you get to the oasis, it dried up. Situation becomes critical as you find yourself in emergency situation. Emergency cry becomes imminent. This is liken to the situation of the widow whose two sons were to be taken away as a result of the debt incurred by her husband to creditors. This woman faced three major problems- recent loss of her darling husband, high poverty level, and slave masters on her neck. Read 2 kings 4:1-7

Before she met Elisha the prophet, the world seems bigger than God. She was confused, and couldn't know what to do. Elisha made us to believe that at times, the only way out in such critical time is to believe and cry to God in faith and in prayer. The answer Elisha provided for this woman was unique. "Little shall become greater only by turning to God alone"

The widow and her two sons, are to carry out the prophets instruction to go for more jars from neighbours, lock themselves inside and pour the little oil she have into the jars until every jar is filled. They did and it paid off.

They were to be alone with God, for they were not dealing with laws of nature, nor human government, nor the church, nor the priesthood, or with the great prophets of God. They should hang on to God alone, in touch with the fountain of miracles.

In time of emergency, you need a secret chamber of isolation in prayer and faith. Every soul must enter it for fruitfulness. By doing this, you are not only isolating human connection which they may boast of later by saying. "If not for me, he won't be somebody today". Rather, glue yourself to the Almighty. The fact is, there are times and places where God will form a mysterious wall around us, and cut away all human support, and all ordinary ways of doing things, and shut us up to something divine, which is utterly new and unexpected, something that old circumstance doesn't fit into. Yes, God perfects his emergency where we do not know just what will happen. Our Lord is super natural, cutting the cloth of our lives on a new pattern, where he makes us look to himself. He shuts in where all we know is that God has hold of us, and is dealing with us, and our expectation is from him alone. At such point, God arise to meet our emergency needs. In emergency, God often makes the sweetest discovery of himself.

Dear brethren, are you in some great trouble? Have you had some great disappointment, have you met some sorrow, some unspeakable loss? Are you in a hard place? Cheer up! You are shut up to faith. Take your trouble the right way. Commit it to God. There will be blessings, help, and revelations of God that will come to you that never could otherwise have come, and many besides yourself will receive great light and blessing because you were shut up to faith. Waiting on God brings to us our journey quicker than our feet.

When you look at the world bigger than God, it means you never discover or know you are a soldier of Christ. The earlier you discover, better. God is at work, and he wants you to know you are Christ Soldier. As a soldier, he takes away your comforts and privileges to make you the better Christian. The Lord always trains his soldiers, not by letting them lie on feather beds, but turning them out, and using them to forced marches and hard service. Take Paul as example, he had imprisonments and pains, sacrifice and suffering. He forgot the world and focus on heaven. He is a soldier of Christ indeed.

God trains soldiers in a hard way. He makes them ford through streams, and swim through rivers, and climb mountains, and walk many a long march with heavy load of sorrow on their backs. This is the way in which he makes them soldiers- not by dressing them up in fine uniforms, to walk about in barracks or to be fine gentlemen in the eyes of men.

God knows that soldiers are only to be made in battle; they are not to be grown in peaceful times. Equip yourself as a soldier and warrior in battle. Do what qualifies a warrior in battles. They are really educated by the smell of powder, in the midst of whizzing bullets and roaring cannonades, not in soft and peaceful times.

In the midst of this, God shall bring out grace and make you grow. He shall develop in you the quality of a soldier and warrior by throwing you into the heart of battle. It is such time you call emergency. God sees you and know how to handle the situation. The world cannot be bigger than God; he is the creator of all things, so he shall handle it well.

PRAYER POINTS

1. Lord Jesus, let me survive all battles by your power and support.

2. I put on armour of God against all odds in the name of Jesus.

3. O Lord, make me a warrior and warlord in the battle of life.

4. No whizzing bullets shall consume me in the battle of life in the name of Jesus.

5. No roaring cannonades shall kill me in the battle of life, in the name of Jesus.

6. O Lord, give me grace that will make me grow, in the name of Jesus.

7. Heat of battle warming up to consume me, my life is not your candidate, expire in the name of Jesus.

8. The world that snare at me, you are not bigger than God, therefore, obey me and carry out my instruction in the name of Jesus.

9. In the battle of life dark river shall not consume me in the name of Jesus.

10. Every mountain before me, disappear in the name of Jesus.

11. O Lord, give me wisdom to handle each situation in every emergency time or period in the name of Jesus.

12. O Lord, make me a soldier of Christ in the name of Jesus.

13. Lord's prophet, appear in my life, in the name of Jesus.

14. Battles of life that consume others shall not consume me, in the name of Jesus.

15. Soldiers of God, guide me 24 hours every day by the power in the name of Jesus.

16. O Lord, set me free from spiritual prison, in the name of Jesus.

17. My sacrifice and suffering shall not be in vain, in the name of Jesus.

18. I surrender comfort and privileges around me, to be a better Christian in the name of Jesus.

19. My troubles, I surrender you to God, quit my life, in the name of Jesus.

20. My faith, grow like mustard seed, in the name of Jesus.

21. Every arrow of poverty fired into my life, come out, backfire in the name of Jesus.

22. Every arrow of sorrow fired into my life, come out, backfire in the name of Jesus.

23. Every arrow of disappointment fired into my life, come out, backfire in the name of Jesus.

24. I recover the loss of past mistakes, in the name of Jesus.

25. Old habit and ways of life that makes me stagnant, die in the name of Jesus.

26. O Lord, open my eyes to new visions and ideas of success, in the name of Jesus.

27. O Lord, appear in my situation of emergency time of need, in the name of Jesus.

28. O Lord, turn my life around and replace helpers that boast of help they rendered, in the name of Jesus.

29. Every human connection that lead to nothing, break in the name of Jesus.

30. O Lord, take me to your seat chamber of fruitfulness in the name of Jesus.

31. Every wicked broadcast assign to pull me down, backfire in the name of Jesus.

32. Evil arresters of good things assign to make me poor, die in the name of Jesus.

33. Every witchcraft handwriting against my life, I wipe you with the blood of Jesus.

CHAPTER FIVE

WHEN IN SORROW…CALL JOHN 14

Storm of life either makes or mar you. Some storms come suddenly in form of great sorrow, bitter disappointment, or a crushing defeat. They seal the forward march of victims, silence hope or introduce stagnancy in a life. Storms either come slowly or furious in nature, those that come slowly appear as trouble that seems so insignificant, but spread wildly un-noticed until it covers the sky and overwhelms.

Brethren, have you been in the storms and swept by the blasts? The answer is, God knows best of the 'sorrow' of life. Does the 'sorrow storm' left you broken, weary, beaten in the valley, or have they lifted you to the sunlit summits of a richer, deeper more abiding manhood and womanhood? The truth is there is no storm that can uproot or kill the tree God knows. No lightening, thunderbolt, beating rain or hurricane can destroy the tree God knows. You are the tree God knows; therefore fear not, no storm shall swallow you. Amen.

Sorrow respects nobody, it cuts across the strata of life, be you young or old, rich or poor, fat or slim; your colour doesn't stop sorrow from visiting. If sudden death hits a family, it is a sign of sorrow. When a family loses the breadwinner of a home, sorrow clouds the house. When a person loses his source of income, job or calling, sorrow follow suits.

Sorrow is a word no one bargains for in the course of life. Sorrow is loaded with negatives and confusion. It is a course of grief, sadness and regret. There is no one in state of sorrow that laughs. Even if he laughs, suddenly cries follows. Such laugh only goes straight to wake and burst warehouse or cry in the belly. Before you know it, there is burst of cry. I pray, this shall not be your portion.

When God wants to make a man he puts him into a storm. The history of mankind is always rough and rugged. David spent part of his better life as a shepherd and in battles. John the Baptist was in the wilderness, with no clothes on but a leather girdle around him. Our Lord Jesus went into forty days and night fasting, yet was tempted by Satan. Moses was forty years as shepherd in the wilderness of Midian, yet when he was sent to release the Israelites it was battle with Pharaoh. Of the desert experience? He was met with furious accusations of brethren he champion into freedom!

All these are enough to bring sorrow into a life but they all managed their circumstances well. No man is made until he has been out into the surge of the storm and seeks the face of the Lord. What you call sorrow may be the handwork of God. What more? The beauties of nature come after the storm. The rugged beauty of the mountain is born in a storm, and the heroes of life are the storm-swept and battle-sacred.

No good comes easy; you must pass through battles of life to realize goodness. In the process, trials and sorrows are met on the way. As soldiers show their scars and talk of battles when they come at last home, so are men and women discuss what they pass through in their daily endeavours. In every tribulation try and press hard to be Christ like. Sorrow is one of the cups of tea we must drink from. Where there is no cross there can't be crown.

Where were you wounded? Where were you insulted? Where were you slapped? Where were lies spoken against you? These are source of sorrow, scars of sorrow that builds one for greater height. God will not look you over for medals, degrees or diplomas, but for scars! There is compensation in every sorrow, and the sorrow is working out the compensation.

Would you like to be there and see yourself pointed at as the one saint who never knew sorrow? Oh no! For you would be an alien in the midst of the sacred brotherhood. Don't lose hope but forge ahead, we shall soon wear the crown and wave the palm!

Are you ready to wave the palm on the last day? You need courage to do this. There are bible passages that fire courage in men and women. Let's look at them one at a time.

Psalm 30:5. **"Weeping may endure for a night, but joy cometh in the morning"**.

2 King 20:5. **"I have heard thy prayer, I have seen thine tears"**.

Isaiah 53:4. **"He hath borne our griefs, and carried out sorrows".**

Job 11:16. **"Thou shalt forget misery, and remember it as waters that pass away".**

Psalm 30:11. **"Thou put off my sackcloth and girded me with gladness".**

Isaiah 49:13 **"Sing… be joyful… break forth into singing; for the Lord hath comforted his people… his afflicted".**

Isaiah 54:11 **"O thou afflicted … and not comforted, behold, I will lay thy stones with fair colours".**

Isaiah 61:3 **"Sorrow is for ever gone! "Give unto them beauty for ashes, oil of joy for mourning, the garment of praise for spirit of heaviness".**

Psalm 27:10 **"When father and mother forsake me, the Lord will take me up".**

Isaiah 54:10. **"The mountains shall depart ... but my kindness shall not depart from thee".**

Psalm 34:18. **"The Lord is nigh unto them that are of a broken heart"**

Luke 6:21. **"Blessed are those that weep now, for ye shall laugh".**

I pray your weep shall not last long but turn to laughter, singing and praises. Amen.

PRAYER POINTS

1. Every storm of life targeted at me scatter in the name of Jesus.
2. Storm of sorrow fashioned against my life, scatter in the name of Jesus.

3. Storm of bitter disappointment against my life, scatter in the name of Jesus.

4. Every crushing defeat around me scatter in the name of Jesus.

5. Every storm of life assign to introduce sorrow to my life, scatter in the name of Jesus.

6. Crown of sorrow assign for me in the spirit, catch fire, and roast to ashes in the name of Jesus.

7. Every sorrow storm assign to break me down, die in the name of Jesus.

8. My place of stay in the valley, I reject you, in the name of Jesus.

9. I move higher and occupy mountain top seat of life, in the name of Jesus.

10. I walk out of sorrow storm that left me broken, weary and beaten in the name of Jesus.

11. Sorrow of life, disappear, riches of life, appear in the name of Jesus.

12. Every thunder bolt assign to scatter my destiny, backfire and kill your sender in the name of Jesus.

13. Every beating rain that introduce sorrow to life, stop by fire, in the name of Jesus.

14. Hurricane of darkness assign against my destiny, die in the name of Jesus.

15. Any power assign to unseat me in my office, die in the name of Jesus.

16. Arrow of sudden death fired against my family, backfire in the name of Jesus.

17. Arrow of darkness fired to kill breadwinner of my family, backfire in the name of Jesus.

18. Every gang up against my source of income scatter in the name of Jesus.

19. Sorrow and confusion looking for where to reside, my house is not for you, die in the name of Jesus.

20. Grief and lamentation, my life is not for you, quit me and die in the name of Jesus.

21. I will not live a life of sadness and regret in the name of Jesus.

22. I shall laugh and not be in sorrow in the name of Jesus.

23. Warehouse of cry in my belly, disappear and rise no more, in the name of Jesus.

24. Burst of cry of sorrow shall not be my portion of my family in the name of Jesus.

25. O Lord, free me in the face of storm in the name of Jesus.

26. O Lord, turn my cross to crown, in the name of Jesus.

27. Strange tongues against me, cliff to the roof of your mouth, in the name of Jesus.

28. Every weep that endure the night in my life, shall lead me to joy in the morning, in the name of Jesus.

29. O Lord, let my prayer and tears meet your mercy, and bless me in the name of Jesus.

30. All misery in my life, be like water that pass me by in the name of Jesus.

31. Sorrow is forever gone! I say bye Amen.

CHAPTER SIX

IF YOU WANT TO BE FRUITFUL...CALL JOHN 15

The book of Ezekiel 34:6 says, **"I will cause the shower to come down in his season, there shall be showers of blessing"**

Brethren, what season are you? Is it, season of drought? Then that is the season for showers. Is it, season for showers? The Lord promises 'a shower of blessings', the word is in the plural. This means, all kinds of blessings God will send. He shall multiply you in the North, South, and West and as well in the East. Everywhere you turn shall be abode of blessings. All God's blessings go together like links in a golden chain. God can transform your thorn into flower. Don't forget, Job got the sunshine after the rain.

Fruitfulness lies in your hands. When a shipwright builds a vessel, does he build it to keep it upon the stocks? Never, he builds it for the sea and storm. He takes both into consideration before he can get a buyer. When making it, he thought of tempests and hurricanes, if he did not, he was poor shipbuilder.

Are you threatened with weeps and cries? Believing your shelter is gone? Or that every rough wind will blow upon you? And every storm will seek to uproot you in the midst of emergency? In every situation you face God shall appear, the Omnipresent God shall come to your aid. The sun of glory shall shine upon you. Heavenly shower shall fall upon thee in more copious abundance than before. Now you shall have favour and love from all. Men and women shall seek to favour you. Your coast shall expand and increase. Your beauty shall attract many, in the name of Jesus.

In the face of harsh weather, don't give up. God capitalize on emergencies to prove himself. At the point you lose hope, God vibrates. At the point you count unfruitful, he pours down rain of blessings. You may be at the end of your strength that is where God appears. God had to bring Abraham to the end of his strength, and let him see that in his own body he could do nothing. He had to consider his own as good as dead, and then take God for the whole work, and when he looked away from himself, and trusted God alone, he won the race against unfruitfulness.

This day nobody wants to pass through testing room of suffering. We want everything to come easy, done easy, and harvested easy. To make us strong, God need to make us pass through his testing room of suffering. He wants a storm-beaten oak, strong enough to withstand storms of life. He wants us to be like granite rocked, withstanding the fierce storms. To make us such, he makes us pass through his testing room of suffering. It is in time of emergency, God cast us into crumbles to try our gold, and to separate it from the dross and alloy.

Do things in an orderly manner so that you don't fail but harvest better. We must crawl before we walk, and we must walk before we run. This is the natural development of life. Never run ahead of yourself; you will never make it. Another thing is that we must learn to crawl and to run – and for this we need the help of others.

Is mediocrity the law of your existence? Are your days remarkable for nothing but sameness and stagnancy? But, I encourage you for greatness. Really, you may not be a genius, have no brilliant gifts or known for any special faculty. There is fruitfulness in your voice. Millions want to listen to you. John the Baptist did no miracle, but Jesus said that among those born of women there had not appeared a greater man than he. John's main business was to bear witness to the light, and this may be yours and mine. Be willing to be only a voice, heard but not seen.

Cry for heavenly fruitfulness and blessings. Jacob wrestled with Angel of covenant and experience fruitfulness. In the night battle dream, it was God in human form pressing and pressing out the old Jacob life. As morning broke, God has prevailed and Jacob fell with his thigh dislocated. But as he fell, he fell into the arms of God, and there he clung and wrestled, too, until the blessing came. New life was born of him. He rose from the earthly to the heavenly, the human to the divine, the natural to the supernatural, and the ordinary to the extra-ordinary. He was called no more Jacob, but Israel. The lesson is, you achieve fruitfulness in the midst of difficult surroundings, deep trial, impossible situation, trying place etc. There comes a crisis hour to each of us.

Do you know the secret of the day blessings and fruitfulness? It is Morning Prayer. Give God the blossom of the day. Let morning be the time you fixed for meeting him. Let the morning be as a cluster of rich grapes, crush and drink sacred wine that gives strength and hope for the day. Successful is the day whose first victory was won in prayer.

Our lives must be quiet and restful if we would see God and hear him whisper to us. He is always whispering to us, only we do not hear, because of the noise, hurry, and distraction which life causes as it rushes on. Learn from the fact, the troubled surface of a lake will not reflect on object. We must wait upon the Lord before we can see vision. Vision of God always transforms human life.

The vision of God transformed Gideon from a coward into a valiant soldier. The vision of Christ changed Thomas from a doubting follower into a loyal, devout disciple. In this modern day, and in the past men have had visions. William Carey saw God, and left his shoemaker's bench and went to Indian. David Livingstone saw God, and left all to follow God through the jungles of dark Africa. Scores and hundreds have had visions of God, and are today in the uttermost parts of the earth. This is fruitfulness.

PRAYER POINTS

1. Lord Jesus, give me vision to know what to do in life, in the name of Jesus.
2. Every obstacle that stands between me and breakthrough, scatter in the name of Jesus.
3. Every idea in me, turn to fruitfulness in the name of Jesus.
4. My breakthrough bring comfort today, in the name of Jesus.
5. I occupy the unoccupied fruitful land and claim it, in the name of Jesus.

6. I claim every unclaimed territory of divine promise in the name of Jesus.

7. O Lord, quicken my steps and desire for the things of heaven, in the name of Jesus.

8. I receive power to rise up with wings as eagles, in the name of Jesus.

9. I claim progress and success in everything I do, in the name of Jesus.

10. I cancel season of failure and frustration targeted at me, in the name of Jesus.

11. O Lord, open my eyes to great ideas and adventures of life, in the name of Jesus.

12. O Lord, let your shower come down in season in the name of Jesus.

13. Every season of drought in my life be converted to season of breakthrough in the name of Jesus.

14. O Lord, let rain of success come forth after black clouds in heaven in the name of Jesus.

15. O Lord, multiply the works of my hands to success in the name of Jesus.

16. O Lord, let my sunshine come after the rain in the order of Job.

17. I subdue and kill agents of darkness against my success in the name of Jesus.

18. Every storm design to scatter my breakthrough be silenced in the name of Jesus.

19. Sea of darkness assign to swallow my virtues, dry up in the name of Jesus.

20. Every rough wind blowing against me, seize, in the name of Jesus.

21. O Lord, appear and save me in every situation in the name of Jesus.

22. Sun of glory above shine upon me in the name of Jesus.

23. O Lord, let your favour and of men be my portion in the name of Jesus.

24. O Lord, let my coast expand in all routs in the name of Jesus.

25. O Lord Jesus, wear me garment of favour and mercy to attract good things and helpers, in the name of Jesus.

26. O Lord, appear in my life, where I am weak in the name of Jesus.

27. O Lord, bless me as you bless Abraham in the name of Jesus.

28. I shall not die in the testing room of suffering in the name of Jesus.

29. Every spirit of stagnancy in my life die in the name of Jesus.

30. O Lord, promote me from ordinary level to extra-ordinary level in the name of Jesus.

31. As from today, anywhere I go, I will find favour in the name of Jesus.

32. Every record of darkness working against my prosperity catch fire and roast to ashes in the name of Jesus.

CHAPTER SEVEN

IF YOU ARE DEPRESSED…CALL PSALM 27

Your trying time is not a killing time. Trials and pressures are among instruments that revive the soul. Really, trials and hard places are needed to press forward. The pressure of hard places makes us value life. Every time we learn from such trials and pressures, we learn better how much life is worth. It makes us to understand the trial of others and fit us to help and sympathize with them.

Are you losing hope as if all is gone? Does it seem everything around you is dark operating without result? Have you gotten to a place where it seems dark? But then, there is hope, all is not lost. Look unto God who caused the sea all night to go back for the children of Israel to pass through. Look unto Jesus, who healed the woman with issue of blood. Look unto God, who transformed bareness to fruitfulness in the life of Sarah.

Let's build attitude of trust. When the wife is married, she at once falls into a new attitude, and acts in accordance with the fact. When we take Christ as our Saviour, as our Sanctifier, as our Healer, or as our Deliverer, out of depression, he expects us to fall into the attitude of recognizing him in the capacity that we have claimed and trust.

In the face of depression, don't be discouraged or timid that a little obstacle depresses and frightens you, walking around it instead of facing it to achieve solution. Pay as little attention to discouragement as possible, either rough or smooth, rain or shine, you shall make it.

Trials and pressures mustn't turn us from prayer. Every depression we encounter must be countered with prayer, believing our prayer is answered.

Every right prayer to our situation is answered before the prayer itself is finished. As God's word cannot fail, whenever we meet those simple conditions in prayer, the answer to our prayer has been granted and completed in heaven as we pray, even though it is showing forth on earth may not occur until long afterward.

Have you not ever heard or seen men and women, town or villages, cities or nations, some disaster drove to a great act of prayer, and by and by the disaster was forgotten. In the act of prayer, the winds blew and the rain fell, windows of heaven open. Things suddenly changed, laughter burst in their mouths.

Lightening that caused fear was gone, thunder was silent of threat, clouds of confusion disappeared. What more? Retreating storm changed form, it threw a scarf of rainbows over its shoulder and neck, and looked back and smile, saying, "The storm is over". The storm withdraws and passed out of sight. The fact is, God may not give us an easy journey to the Promised Land, but he will give us a safe one.

Don't lie low when depressed. There are instruments to apply to kill pains and resurrect to life as champion. One of such is to sing praises to God. It opens doors of opportunities. It heals old wounds and makes heart merry.

We can sing our cares away easier than we can reason them away. Sing in the morning. The birds are the earliest to sing, and birds are more without care than anything else that I know of. Sing at evening. Singing is the last thing that Robbins – that small, brownish bird with red breast-feathers do. When they have done their daily work, when they have flown their last flight, and picked up their last morsel of food, then on a topmost of bush plant, they sing praise of song. Learn to sing, let song touch all the way through to escape depression.

Don't doubt God; don't grieve him by doubting his love. Yet lift up your head, and begin to praise him even now for deliverance which is on the way to you, and you will be abundantly rewarded for the delay which has tried your faith. We never know where God hides his pools. We see a rock, and we cannot guess it is the home of the spring. Things may seem to be going all wrong, but he knows as well as we, and he will rise in the right moment if we really trust him so fully as to let him work in his own way and time.

PRAYER POINTS

1. My trying time shall not consume me, in the name of Jesus.
2. O Lord, convert my trials to triumph in the name of Jesus.

3. O God arise in my favour, convert my scars to stars in the name of Jesus.

4. O God arise in my favour, convert my failure to success in the name of Jesus.

5. O God arise in my favour, convert my defeat to victory in the name of Jesus.

6. O God arise in my favour, convert my poverty to prosperity in the name of Jesus.

7. O God arise in my favour, convert my temptation to triumph in the name of Jesus.

8. O God arise in my favour, convert my frustration to fulfillment in the name of Jesus.

9. O Lord arise in my favour, convert my disgrace to grace in the name of Jesus.

10. O God arise in my favour, convert my weakness to strength in the name of Jesus.

11. O God arise in my favour, convert my disappointment to appointment in the name of Jesus.

12. I receive anointing of excellence to shine above others, in the name of Jesus.

13. O Lord, plant me by the river of prosperity to shine and bring forth fruits in the name of Jesus.

14. Every darkness around me clear away in the name of Jesus.

15. Spiritual blindness in my life, clear away in the name of Jesus.

16. Prayer less spirit in my life die in the name of Jesus.

17. My hope is not lost, Jesus is with me.

18. Every Red Sea on my way to the Promise Land, dry up in the name of Jesus.

19. Depression and fear in my heart, vanish in the name of Jesus.

20. Health hazards in my life be converted to wealth of health in the name of Jesus.

21. Every bareness in my life be fruitful and multiply in the name of Jesus.

22. O Lord, heal me of every infirmity in the name of Jesus.

23. I walk to the gate of my enemy and possess it in the name of Jesus.

24. Whether it rains or shine, rough or smooth, I shall make it in the name of Jesus.

25. Trials and pressures shall turn me from prayer warrior to prayer warlord in the name of Jesus.

26. Every disaster assign for me scatter and be converted to joy in the name of Jesus.

27. Windows of heaven open to my life, in the name of Jesus.

28. Laughter shall not leave my mouth, I shall laugh and dance to the glory of God.

29. Every lightening and thunder that cause fear in my life, stop by fire.

30. Wasters assign against me be wasted in the name of Jesus.

31. Powers assign to oppress me in the spirit, die in the name of Jesus.

32. Agenda of darkness for my life scatter in the name of Jesus.

33. I declare today, "The storm is over" in the name of Jesus.

CHAPTER EIGHT

IF YOUR POCKET BOOK IS EMPTY ... CALL PSALM 37

Our trials are at times doors to great opportunities. Too often we look on them as great obstacles. Every difficult situation is one of God's chosen ways of proving to us his love and care. It is then every cloud becomes a rainbow, every mountain a path of accession. When we look back upon the past, it is when God wants to give us the richest blessing.

There are people and things that threaten to bar our progress in the divine life. Those heavy claims, that challenging occupation, that thorn in the flesh, that daily cross etc., are what champion setbacks in life. These are mountains we pray to leave for us to excel. But you know what? These are the very conditions of achievements. Life is not full of roses; you must have a cross in your path. It is said, "No event, no history". Obstacles and trials you meet in your path are events of life. They have been put into our lives as the means to the very graces and virtues for which we have been praying so long. Trial doesn't mean failure is on the way or to test worthiness but to increase your worth and resilience. The oak is not only tested by the storms, but roughened by them.

God is never in a haste, he appears at the right time. Be assured that if God waits longer than you could wish, it is only to make the blessing doubly precious. God waited four thousand years, till the fullness of time, before he sent his Son. Our time is in his hands, he will avenge his elect speedily. He will do it right and not delay one hour too long.

It is in emergency we need God most, but he is a wise husbandman, who waits for precious time. He cannot gather the fruit till it is ripe. He is not anxious to do things. He knows when we are spiritually ready to receive the blessing to our profit and his glory. Waiting in the sunshine of his love is what will ripen the soul of his blessings. Waiting under the cloud of trial that breaks in showers of blessings is as needful. God's river, which is full of water, shall burst its banks, and pour upon us a tide of wealth and grace.

At the point pocket is empty, you are disturbed in the heart. You look as if you can't co-ordinate issues. It is as useless to oneself. Self-dignity dwindle, bitter complains fill the mouth.

The love of our father has no limit, his grace has no measure. He knows when the pocket is empty; he knows how to fill it. When we reach the end of our resources, our father's full giving is only begun. Abounding grace rests with him. He gives more grace when the burden grows greater. He sends more strength when the labour increases. He doesn't leave us to circumstances. He is always with us. He jettisons afflictions by his mercy and nullifies trials by multiplied peace.

Be hopeful in the face of empty pocket; when bank account goes red; when close to nothing is at home to fall back on. Take good looks of characters in the Bible. It is Job in the tempest, it is Abraham on the road to Mariah, it is Moses in the desert of Midian, it is the Son of man in the Garden of Gethsemane.

You shall reach the climax of strength when you learn to wait for hope. Our God still have the windows in heaven. They are yet in service to mankind. The bolts slide as easily as of old. The hinges have not grown rusty. Be hopeful, our God shall fling them open, than keep them shut and hold back. When windows are open, they perform various functions. He opened it for Moses and the sea parted. He opened windows for the Israelites in the desert, manna and quail came down. He opened it for Joshua, and Jordan rolled back. He opened it for Gideon, and host fled.

Heaven is the same rich storehouse as of old. The treasure rooms are still full of gifts waiting for us to possess. The fountains and streams still overflow. The lack is not on God's side. Therefore, ask Big. Don't be like the man who asks for a cupful and the ocean remains; or one who ask for a sunbeam and the sun abides. Don't let your asking falls short of the father is giving. He can provide.

To pray for full pocket connotes ability to solve problems as it arises. Therefore, don't pray for easy life. Pray to be stronger men and women that handle situations as they arise. Rather, pray for powers equal to your tasks. It is such power that handles tasks. What more at this point, the doing of your work shall be no miracle, but you shall be a miracle.

Pray, for the grace is bountifully available to you. The book of second Corinthians 12:9 says, **"My grace is** (not shall be or may be**) sufficient for thee"**. Live in the reality of this message that the grace of the Lord is sufficient for you. It is sufficient already, claim it and love it, so that your pocket may be full.

The lesson here is this; never turn God's facts into hopes, or prayers, but simply use them as realities, and you will find them powerful as you believe them. If a man is poor, who is to blame? Christ puts the key of the treasure chamber into our hand, and bids us to take all that we want. If a man is admitted into the billion vault of a bank, and told to help himself and comes out with a penny or a kobo or a cent, whose fault is it that he is poor? It is never fault of God. Christians at times have scanty free riches of God.

You are the child of a king, claim your right from Him, don't doubt whether they belong to you. It is your privilege as child of the Royal Family. Demand your right, claim it by fire!

I pray, your storehouse shall not be empty. What you lost in the past, shall be restored to you seven fold, in the name of Jesus.

PRAYER POINTS

1. O Lord, let my trials be doors of great opportunities in the name of Jesus.
2. Every obstacle on my way become my stepping stone to breakthrough in the name of Jesus.
3. Poverty that leads to heart attack, my life is not your candidate, clear away in the name of Jesus.
4. My source of wealth shall not dry in the name of Jesus.
5. My burden grows greater, O Lord, lighten and destroy it by fire.

6. Every affliction in my life, die in the name of Jesus.

7. Every trial in my life be nullified by multiple peace in the name of Jesus.

8. Every leaking hole in my pocket be sealed with the blood of Jesus.

9. O Lord, let abounding grace rest on me, in the name of Jesus.

10. I will not fail and die in hardship in the name of Jesus.

11. O Lord, make me a prosperous child of God, in the name of Jesus.

12. I shall not live a wasteful or extravagant life in the name of Jesus.

13. Alliances of witches and wizards against my prosperity, scatter in the name of Jesus.

14. Wicked covenant against me break in the name of Jesus.

15. O Lord, prove yourself in my finance in the name of Jesus.

16. Lord's river of breakthrough, full, burst your banks and gives me great wealth in the name of Jesus.

17. Owner of evil load, carry your load in the name of Jesus.

18. Heavenly strength come to my life and strengthen me in the name of Jesus.

19. Satanic opposition against my life, scatter in the name of Jesus.

20. I smash every plan of Satan against me in the name of Jesus.

21. I plant seed of success of great testimonies in the name of Jesus.

22. Every cloud in my life become rainbow of great expectation and fulfillment of God's promise for my life.

23. Every wall of darkness keeping me solitary be pulled down in the name of Jesus.

24. Every embargo placed upon me scatter in the name of Jesus.

25. Everything that makes progress impossible in my life, die in the name of Jesus.

26. Every mountain in my life become plain in the name of Jesus.

27. O Lord, give me strength to defeat every cross that comes my way, in the name of Jesus.

28. O Lord, appear at the right time in my life, in the name of Jesus.

29. O Lord, I am your elect avenge speedily in the name of Jesus.

30. O Lord, let the fruit of my labour ripe for harvest now in the name of Jesus.

31. I am a child of the King; I shall not die poor in the name of Jesus.

32. I receive key of treasure chamber in the name of Jesus.

33. The grace of the Lord is sufficient for me, in the name of Jesus.

CHAPTER NINE

IF YOU ARE LOSING CONFIDENCE IN PEOPLE…CALL 1 CORINTHIANS 13

Confidence abound when everything goes the way expected. Loss of confidence starts when equilibrium position is negative or goes down ward, and or when one experiences digression in activities. At this point confidence is lost, valley life sets in while dividends dwindles, leading to hopelessness. Loss of confidence can arise among spouse, neighbours or friend, in office, in business or in the house of God.

To lose confidence is an approach to negatives, suspicion, loss etc. Valley life may set in that makes you love wrong thoughts and songs of low heart. There are songs which can only be learned in the valley. No art can teach you, no rules of voice can make you perfectly sing. It is the experience of the past you put in place that turns to songs. Music is in the heart. It is written in the heart and comes to play in series. They are songs of memory, of personal experience. You knew better, experience better and can put to song better. Here you are losing confidence. This is emergency that begs for succor and encouragement from people and self. It is as if in the valley and need a way of escape. To escape you bring out burden from the shadow of the past and mount on the wings of yesterday to forge ahead in spirit.

At this point you shall be involved in boldness and hope. You shall be involved in songs of triumph, in hymn of victory to Christ who can set you free. He is the only one who can restore you to confidence you are losing. He is the one who can set you free from the memory of the chain.

The sense of triumph must come to stay. In this situation all you need is to rely on Jesus. It is you that will sing song of redemption, song of victory, song of liberty etc. no angel or archangel can sing it so sweetly as you can. To sing it as you sing it, they must pass through what your frustrations and sorrows are and this they cannot do.

Let's place confidence in God even in the darkest hour. Learn to trust in the name of the Lord and rely upon him. He knows the way out of the woods. Let us climb up into his arms, and trust him to take us out by the shortest and surest road. The first thing to do is, do nothing. This is hard for poor human nature to do. It is said, "When you are rattled, don't rush" meaning, "When you don't know what to do, don't do it"

Is anything too hard for the Lord? Genesis 18:14. Here is God's loving challenge for you and to me. He wants us to think of the deepest, highest, worthiest desire and longing of our hearts, something which perhaps was our desire, for ourselves or for someone dear to us, yet which has been so long unfulfilled that we have looked upon it as only a lost desire, that which might have been but now cannot be, and so have given up hope of seeing it fulfilled in this life.

Don't lose hope, rather build faith. The Father is training you, how to leave school of sorrow. Emergency is not peculiar to only you. He sends the situation to prove thee, to educate thee, and to train thee for the end time. Cry may come at night, yet it shall not consume thee, rather, laughter shall be found in your mouth. Your voice shall be turned to sweet melody. There shall be light at the end of the tunnel.

Are the shadows dark and long? Fear not, build hope. Ask Jesus to come close beside you. He will give you a new sweet song. He will give it and sing it with you, so that you don't experience loneliness or lose confidence in your pursuits and in God.

In the face of frustration and calamity, be confident. What you call emergency may mean door of heaven wants to open. When Jacob ran for his dear life like the exiled, he laid himself down in the desert place to sleep, and in his dreams appear a ladder which united heaven with earth and at the top stood God.

John was in the Isle of Patmos, alone, rockery, inhospitable prison, for the Word of God and the testimony of Jesus. It was under such circumstance, separated from all loved ones of Ephesus; debarred from the worship of Church, condemned to the companionship of uncongenial fellow – captives, a door was opened. He wrote the book of Revelation.

Pray to God for confidence and strength. Tell God to send and equip you with strength. Pray to God for strength of character which makes everything in life work with ease. We need continuous strength with reserves of power that cannot exhaust. Pray for strength; strength of will, strength of affection, strength of judgment, strength of ideas and strength of achievement.

PRAYER POINTS

1. O Lord, reveal the bad habits among my friends and relatives to me, in the name of Jesus.

2. Those that trust me for evil O Lord, expose them in the name of Jesus.

3. Evil pot cooking my glory in evil fire break in the name of Jesus.

4. O Lord, replace people I lost confidence in, with people of good character in the name of Jesus.

5. My time-life in the valley expire in the name of Jesus.

6. Thought and songs of sorrow in my heart come to an end in the name of Jesus.

7. Bad memory shall not sink my life, in the name of Jesus.

8. I will not settle down in the valley of life in the name of Jesus.

9. My spirit in the valley what are you doing there, escape, come out and locate me in the name of Jesus.

10. Music in my heart be converted to songs of joy in the name of Jesus.

11. O Lord, let me match on with songs of triumph in the name of Jesus.

12. Boldness to serve my God and love Jesus, fall upon me, in the name of Jesus.

13. I shall triumph over situations that come my way, in the name of Jesus.

14. I refuse to be a candidate in the school of sorrow in the name of Jesus.

15. In the face of frustration and calamity, I will not surrender in the name of Jesus.

16. O Lord, let the angels descend and ascend for my sake in the name of Jesus.

17. Every loneliness in my life, bring testimony in the name of Jesus.

18. O Lord, give me strength of character to excel in life, in the name of Jesus.

19. O Lord, fire me with strength of will to do all things in the name of Jesus.

20. O Lord, give me strength to be loved and love others in the name of Jesus.

21. O Lord, give me strength to judgment, to counsel and handle situation well in the name of Jesus.

22. Holy Spirit, guide my steps in the name of Jesus.

23. I remove my name from the book of no-confident in the name of Jesus.

24. Spirit of failure in my life die in the name of Jesus.

25. Every stronghold of darkness upon my life, die in the name of Jesus.

26. I will sing song of redemption to the glory of the Lord Almighty, in the name of Jesus.

27. I will sing song of victory to the glory of the Lord Almighty, in the name of Jesus.

28. I will sing song of liberty to the glory of the Lord Almighty, in the name of Jesus.

29. I will remember my God, even in the darkest hour in the name of Jesus.

30. I climb unto the arms of Jesus out of the valley, in the name of Jesus.

31. Every cry that come at night shall be followed with laughter in the name of Jesus.

32. O Lord, give me hope, confidence and strength in the name of Jesus.

33. Star hijackers after my life die in the name of Jesus.

CHAPTER TEN

WHEN PEOPLE SEEM UNKIND…CALL JOHN 15

Unkindness is an act of resentment or hatred of people to others. No matter your kindness, everyone won't receive it with joy. Jesus was kind, yet he was hated and crucified for no reason. He showed deep love to mankind, yet he was accused wrongly.

People who are kind to you may suddenly change as a result of progress, achievement or favour you receive from men and God. Let's take the case of the Egyptians and the descendants of Jacob as example. When Joseph was sold into slavery, and eventually became Prime Minister in Egypt, he brought in his family and was accepted with open hands. Because of Joseph, Pharaoh ceded the fertile land of Goshen, on the east side of the Nile Delta to them. This was a place conveniently near to the royal palace at Memphis. There they had settled about 70 in all that time. But that was long ago.

Now, in this warm and prosperous land, that 70 had multiplied many times over, until whole settlements of Jacob's descendants, the Hebrews as the Egyptians called them, had sprung up in the land of Goshen. At this point, these settlements were not regarded favourable by the Egyptians, there once friend and neighbor increasingly resented their presence.

In fact, the new Pharaoh, who came to power long after the era of Joseph, had recently been making speeches which were openly antagonistic. He spoke angry words and believes the Hebrews had been indebted to them for the land that had been ceded to them. The gratitude for Joseph's wisdom during the years of famine suddenly changed. The era of kindness was gone; it is now replaced with unkindness.

The Hebrew who were once loved, are now hated. There is total resentment and unkindness of Egyptians. How seasons change? They could remember when their predecessors were honoured visitors at the palace, their opinion valued and their culture and religion respected. The Hebrew is treated as despised aliens who had multiplied their numbers unacceptably and were to be treated as nothing more than free labour. They were treated unkindly.

The outlook was bleak. They lost respect and status, and suffer daily physical persecution. They felt helpless, victims of circumstance, at the mercy of people who didn't like them, had total power over them and treated them contemptuously.

To us, such times in life are product or consequence of our sin or wrong doing. Unkindness is a product of our hand work. Unkindness is at times as a result of jealousy. Unkindness sow seeds of separation among men. It unleashes terror at times. When people seem unkind to you, you must be on guide. What is worst may happen anytime. An unkind person doesn't thank God of one; he is desperate of doing evil or harm. For the Hebrews, they could see no reason for it. There was simply no justice in it at all. They felt abandoned by their God, not knowing he was already secretly moving towards them.

They cried to God and he answered. By then, in a simple mud hut in the Hebrew settlement in Goshen, a pregnant young woman was carrying in her womb the people's hope. She later delivered a baby boy. The name of the baby was Moses. God used him mightily not only to liberate the

Hebrews, but never to experience unkindness from the Egyptians.

No one experience unkindness and feel happy. What type of unkindness do you experience from people? Why are they antagonistic? Do you have flurs in you? How do you handle issues with people? Do you notice this of recent, or is it a long time issue? What are your reactions as well? These and other questions best known to you need to be answered.

At this point, I advise you read the book of John chapter 15: 1-27. This is the contact point in time of emergency when humiliated with unkindness. The message in this chapter is loaded with message of love and acceptance. Jesus is the vine we must remain in. We are champions in Christ. We can't lose or be thrown aside. Our links with Christ bring joy and favour. You need to be in Christ, or else, you will be exposed in the hands of enemy. You will be like a branch thrown away and withers.

Emergency prayers only ascend to the seat of God, if you remain in his love. Such love includes love to your neighbor. If you love your neighbor, Jesus will not only love you but be your friend. Imagine him being your friend; every unkindness from people shall disappear in you.

Unkindness from people is not new. You are not the first, and shall not be the last. Even when you are kind to people, they pay back with unkindness. The Psalmist says, **"Those who hate me without reason outnumber the hairs of my head; many are my enemies without cause, those who seek to destroy me. I am forced to restore what I did not steal"** Psalm 69:4. This is the lamentation of David before God in the face of hostility.

It is not always easy to do well when surrounded by enemies. You need to live and your eyes wide open, sensitive to your surroundings. It is time we apply emergency key prayers to multiply atmosphere of kindness. When you pray the prayers below, heaven shall open for your sake. Negative atmosphere around you shall evaporate and become void. Wicked gang up against you shall scatter; mouths of blackmailers shall be padlocked by heavenly powers. Those who frown at you shall suddenly apply reverse gear and leave by fire.

The bottom line is, people can be unkind anytime. They can be unkind when you do well. They can be unkind to your success, achievement or breakthrough. They can be unkind without your knowledge. At times, they laugh with you, but inwardly treacherous. You may live in the same house or environment, be in the same establishment or office. They can be close to you or live far away, the bottom line is; they are unkind to you.

PRAYER POINTS

1. Lord Jesus, wear me with garment of love in the name of Jesus.

2. Lord Jesus, wear me with garment of favour in the name of Jesus.

3. Every contrary word spoken against me backfire in the name of Jesus.

4. Those that hate me without cause, O Lord, handle them.

5. Those that I show love but are not happy with me, meet double failure in the name of Jesus.

6. Every garment of hatred in my body, I pull you off in the name of Jesus.

7. Those who accept me with open hands shall not turn against me in the name of Jesus.

8. What people give to me free shall not work against me in the name of Jesus.

9. Those that plan to pull me down at pinnacle of progress die in the name of Jesus.

10. Those assign to remove my ladder of progress from my legs, die in the name of Jesus.

11. Any power assign to unseat me, you are a failure, die in the name of Jesus.

12. My crown of glory shall not be taken away in the name of Jesus.

13. My prosperity shall not draw me to untimely grave in the name of Jesus.

14. Friends and neighbours that suddenly hated me, my God shall flog you, in the name of Jesus.

15. Those who make open criticism of me without cause, O Lord padlock their mouths, in the name of Jesus.

16. I will not pay debt I do not owe in the name of Jesus.

17. The kindness I do to people shall not work against me in the name of Jesus.

18. Every root of hatred against me wither in the name of Jesus.

19. Those who once love me shall not hate me in the name of Jesus.

20. Spirit of unkindness following me about, die in the name of Jesus.

21. Sudden hatred shall not replace love people have for me in the name of Jesus.

22. I receive honour, I shall not be dishonoured in the name of Jesus.

23. I will not be a servant when I should be treated as King in the name of Jesus.

24. What makes me laugh today shall not make me cry tomorrow in the name of Jesus.

25. My future shall not be bleak in the name of Jesus.

26. Every unkindness as a result of jealously, die in the name of Jesus.

27. Every unkindness as a result of my handwork expire in the name of Jesus.

28. O Lord, as I cry to you answer me in the name of Jesus.

29. Flurs in me causing hatred in my life, die in the name of Jesus.

30. O Lord, give me wisdom to forge ahead in life.

31. Long-time and short-time hatred, die in the name of Jesus.

32. I shall not be treated as branch of good tree, cut, thrown away to wither in the name of Jesus.

33. Evil arrow fired against me wither in the name of Jesus.

34. Those that frown at me apply reverse gear and flee in the name of Jesus.

CHAPTER ELEVEN

IF DISCOURAGED ABOUT YOUR WORK…CALL PSALM 126

Work and work place is our second home. It should be attractive and motivated. It is our source of wealth, it builds future today. Our tomorrow rests there. All mind and energy should be directed to what you do to earn a living. Whatever is opposed to it, affects you. This is the reason every obstacle or barrier on your way must be rebuked to give way.

None the less, discouragement sets in at work. It is difficult not to have, and or, experience non trouble shooting time at place of work, or in career or calling. You should know right words to use, right step to take and right people to meet. Really, God is the ultimate to all question and answer, but he shall use people and circumstances to bring solution.

Jonah was sent as a prophet to Nineveh, that great city to preach the message of God. This message doesn't go well with him. Out of fear and lack of interest, he quietly planned to take a different course. He was a prophet that thought there was somewhere he could get to escape from God.

Instead of him to phone God, he allowed spirit of discouragement to overtake him. He embarked on a wrong journey that nearly caused him his life and that of co-crew. He eventually created a lot of trouble and loss for the boat owners. Rather than be in Tarshih, God took him to his place of assignment and gave him "Second Chance". The Bible records it.

"Now the word of the Lord came to Jonah the second time, saying, "Arise, go to Nineveh, that great city, and preach to it the message that I tell you" Jonah 3:1-2

You shouldn't allow seed of discouragement a place in your life. To be discouraged means, lack of courage, confidence, hope, strength of heart and soul. It also means low or non-moral support from people. A discouraged person is loaded with heaviness in the heart. He needs good word that gladdens the heart. A person with heavy heart is full of bitter soul and weak bones. Words heard either encourage or do otherwise.

In the midst of discouragement, God has many opportunities for you to succeed. Know one thing, when discouragement sets in, God is telling you opportunities are coming ahead. It is you that should phone God to reveal the coming opportunities and how to go about it.

Opportunities that open at the heat of discouragement are many. It may be that God wants to re-build you, adding to your knowledge and wisdom. It may mean God wants to reverse your course. He may have good plan of change in trade or career for you. It may be for better vision by telling you to prepare and leave present pursuits. The bottom line is, in the midst of discouragement, phone God.

When we look at the life of Peter at the eve of his Master's arrest he was discouraged. He was confused and couldn't fathom out, how a great man like Jesus, can be arrested like a common criminal without resistance. With human judgment, Peter denied ever knowing Christ! Before then, he vowed to die with Jesus. Luke 22:33. That was when things were sweet. He later denied Jesus in the face of crucifixion.

This is why, in office you shouldn't be discouraged when your peer, or best friend speak evil of you or deny you before your boss. The subordinate you fight tooth and nail for, in term of promotion or in allied matters may rise up against you. Don't be discouraged. Your boss in office you work with all heart may refuse you promotion or score you low. Don't be discouraged as well

When you phone God, the message you may likely receive is that of hope and assurance. Let these stir up faith and confidence in you. In the midst of discouragement don't belittle yourself. Try and plan big and make room for the impossible. Don't plan on impossibility. Phone God concerning possibility. Give possibility a room in your heart, forge ahead and be a winner.

PRAYER POINTS

1. Any power that laid ambush for me die in your ambush in the name of Jesus.
2. Double fire, double thunder, locate my enemies and kill them in the name of Jesus.

3. Hammer of God break into pieces the head of my enemies in the name of Jesus.

4. Any power of my father's house, assign to pursue me summersault and die in the name of Jesus.

5. Any power of my mother's house, assign to pursue me summersault and die in the name of Jesus.

6. Spirit of Pharaoh that made me a slave in the spirit die in the name of Jesus.

7. Holy Spirit of God open new chapter in my life today in the name of Jesus.

8. Dark powers assign to arrest me die in the name of Jesus.

9. Fire bullet from heavenly, locate unprotected head of my Goliath in the name of Jesus.

10. Every mountain, assign to destroy me; scatter in the name of Jesus.

11. Goliath of my life die, by fire in the name of Jesus.

12. Thou Hamman pursing my Modecia die by fire in the name of Jesus.

13. Thou Jezebel pursuing my Elijah die by fire in the name of Jesus.

14. Thunder of God destroy stronghold holding me captive in the name of Jesus.

15. I slaughter witchcraft animals that swallow my virtues in the name of Jesus.

16. O Lord my God envelop me with heavenly bullet proof in the name of Jesus.

17. No mountain shall arise second time in my life in the name of Jesus.

18. I shall not live a sorrowful life in the name of Jesus.

19. My marriage/destiny shall not scatter in the name of Jesus.

20. My career and destiny shall not scatter in the name of Jesus.

21. Satanic pollution against my destiny disappear in the name of Jesus.

22. My helpers shall not die before they locate me in the name of Jesus.

23. Where is the Lord God of Elijah, kill every affliction in my life in the name of Jesus.

24. Satanic plantation in my life die by fire in the name of Jesus.

25. Bank of darkness assigned to liquidate me catch fire and roast to ashes in the name of Jesus.

26. Every cage assigned to cage me break to pieces in the name of Jesus.

27. Every territorial bondage break by fire in the name of Jesus.

28. Every river of darkness flowing into my life die by fire in the name of Jesus.

YOU HAVE BATTLES TO WIN
TRY THESE BOOKS

1. COMMAND THE DAY

Each day of the week is loaded with meanings and divine assurance. God did not create each day of the week for the fun of it. Blessings, success, gifts, resources, hopes, portfolios, duties, rights, prophecies, warnings and challenges, are loaded in each day.

Do you know the language, command or decree you can use to claim what belongs to you in each day of the week? Do you know in Christendom, Monday can be equated to one of the days of creation in Genesis chapter one? Do you know creation lasted for six days and God rested on the seventh day? What day of the week can Christian equate as the first day of the week, if we follow Christian calendar? What day can we call day seven?

This book shall give insight to these questions. It shall explain how you can command each day of the week according to creation in the book of Genesis chapter one.

2. PRAYER TO REMEMBER DREAMS

A lot of people are passing through this spiritual epidemic on a daily basis. Their dream life is epileptic, having no ability to remember all dreams they dream, or sometimes forget everything entirely. This is nothing but spiritual havoc you need to erase from your spiritual record.

The answer to every form of spiritual blackout caused by spiritual erasers is found in, **PRAYER TO REMEMBER DREAMS.**

3. 100% CONFESSSIONS AND PROPHECIES TO LOCATE HELPERS.

This is a wonderful book on confessions and prophecies to locate helpers and helpers to locate you. It **is a prayer book loaded with over two thousand (2,000) prayer points.**

The book unravels how to locate unknown helpers, prayers to arrest mind of helpers and prayers for manifestation after encounter with helpers.

4. ANOINTING FOR ELEVENTH HOUR HELP.

This book tells much of what to do at injury hour called eleventh hour. When you read and use this book as prescribed fear shall vanish in your life when pursuing a project, career or contract.

5. PRAYER TO LOCATE HELPERS.

Our divine helper is God. He created us to be together and be of help to one another. In the midst of no help we lost out, ending our journey in the wilderness.

There are keys assign to open right doors of life. You need right key to locate your helpers. Enough is enough; of suffering in silence.

With this book, you shall locate your helpers while your helpers shall locate you.

6. GOLIATH AT THE GATE OF MARRIAGE.

Sex violence is rampant worldwide. Rapists carry out evil intents as if nothing will happen. Innocent girls and women are molested by faceless men who refuse to keep their Libido in check. This led to widespread cry from victims of circumstances as laughter and joy is hardly found on faces of ladies in secret and in public.

Unfortunately women are involved. With tricks and false promises, innocent girls are trafficked overseas into prostitution. They caused many destinies to sink as victims could not find their bearings in the cloud they find themselves.

There are ways out of this mess and promising steps to take. This book shall give every family and readers best way to handle every matter relating to sex violence. Obtain this book.

7. SEX IN THE DREAM

Sex in the dream is causing sex havoc in families. Many marriages reap what they least bargain for as a result of sex tyrants that molest them in sleep. These sleep spouse are either called spirit husband or spirit wife. They have sex with victims and cause marriage to collapse.

Their untold hardship on victims brought about the birth of this book loaded with prayers. The book is divided into two parts. Part one gives details of causes, effects and way out of sleep harassment, while part two is loaded with right prayers and prayer points. The book shall also tell you how to recover what you lost as a result of damage done to your destiny in the sleep.

Wake up and grab this book. It is marvelous.

8. SPIRIT OF DOG

This book treats how a particular spirit called Spirit of dog that captivates lives of millions worldwide can be put to check. This spirit is a one that brings shame before you know it. It is a spirit that drains purse and cause widespread promiscuity and diseases at will.

Both young and old, believers and non-believers can be arrested by this faceless spirit which made many mad for sex. This book is marvelous as it gives details of captivities orchestrated by this spirit and how it can be silenced from operating in a life.

Lay your hands on it for good.

9. NAKED WARRIORS.

Many homes, heart of men and women, offices and environs can best be described as palace of immorality. The word immorality means nothing to such people as they swim in pools of destruction. Every immoral act starts from the heart which arrest victim to lust. They are trapped and find it difficult to escape.

But this book is unique as it gives right dose of freedom from this circumstance. It is high time you seek freedom from sexual captivity, promiscuity and lust. By how can this be achieved? Buy this book and experience wonders of God.

10. PRAYER FOR THE FRUIT OF THE WOMB

This prayer book is children magnet. By faith and believe in God Almighty, as soon as you use this book open doors to child bearing shall be yours. Amen

11. PRAYER FOR PREGNANT WOMEN.

This is a spiritual prayer book loaded with prayers of solution for pregnant women. As soon as you take in, the prayers you shall pray from day one of conception to the day of delivery are written in this book.

12. WARFARE IN THE OFFICE

It is high time you pray prayers of power must change hands in office. Use this book and liberate yourself from every form of office yoke.

13. MY MARRIAGE SHALL NOT BREAK

Marriage is corner piece of life, happiness and joy. You need to hold it tight and guide it from wicked intruders and destroyer of homes.

14. FREEDOM FOR TENANTS PARTS 1 & 2

Are you a tenant, Land lord bombarded left and right, front and back by wicked people around you?

With this book you shall be liberated from the hooks of the enemy.

15. DICTIONARY OF DREAMS

This is a must book for every home. It gives accurate details to about **10,000 (Ten thousand) dreams and interpretations,** written in alphabetical order for quick reference and easy digestion. The book portrays spiritual revelations with sound prophetic guidelines. It is loaded with Biblical references and violent prayers.

Ask for yours today.

For Further Enquiries Contact
**THE AUTHOR
EVANGELIST TELLA OLAYERI
P.O. Box 1872 Shomolu Lagos.
Tel: 08023583168**

FROM AUTHOR'S DESK

BEFORE YOU GO

Hello,

Thank you for purchasing this book. Would you consider posting a review about this book? In addition to providing feedback and arousing others into Christ's bosom, reviews can help other customers to know about the book.

Please take a minute to leave a review on this book, no matter how short it is.

I would appreciate that!

Thank you in advance, for your review and your patronage!!

NOTE: You can get all my books from my website www.tellaolayeri.com

GOOD NEWS!!!

My audiobook is now available. To get one go to acx.com and search **Tella Olayeri**.

Thanks.

www.ingramcontent.com/pod-product-compliance
Lightning Source LLC
Chambersburg PA
CBHW052018150726
47999CB00004B/1720